Bet
and

Trevor Millum

- Fern House Books -

Published by Fern House Books
Barrow-upon-Humber DN19 7AA
ISBN 978-0-9955023-0-7
Printed by Ruddocks, Lincoln
01522 529591
martin@ruddocks.co.uk

CONTENTS

INTRODUCTION

This book was inspired by a discovery
in Caistor Heritage Centre: a book by
Pete Skipworth - 'Step into the Lincolnshire Wolds. I liked the way
he had written & illustrated it, and
included the odd poem & observation
in what was mainly a book of walks.
It immediately gave me the idea of
a book of my own, based on the
area between the Wolds & the river,
the places just south of the Humber,
where I've lived for nearly 40 years.
Mine would not be a book of walks,
though it would include a few; it
would have descriptions of as
many of the interesting places along
the Humber as I could fit in, together
with poems I had written over the
years, and line drawings. And
it would all be handwritten....

Barrow-upon-Humber
2016

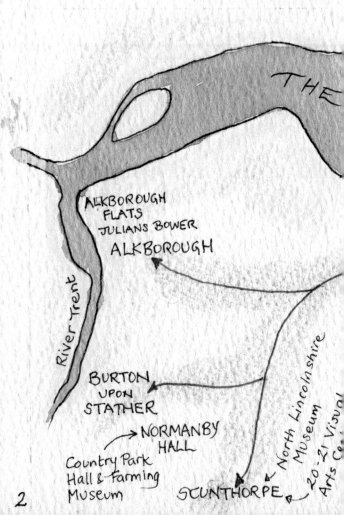

THE

ALKBOROUGH
FLATS
JULIANS BOWER
ALKBOROUGH

River Trent

BURTON
UPON
STATHER

→ NORMANBY
HALL

Country Park
Hall & Farming
Museum

North Lincolnshire
Museum

20-21 Visual
Arts Ce

SCUNTHORPE

2

...ositions of places described

continued

HUMBER
FAR INGS
READS ISLAND
SOUTH FERRIBY
ANCHOLME VALLEY
...e Horkstow
...spension Bridge
BRIGG
Brigg Heritage Centre

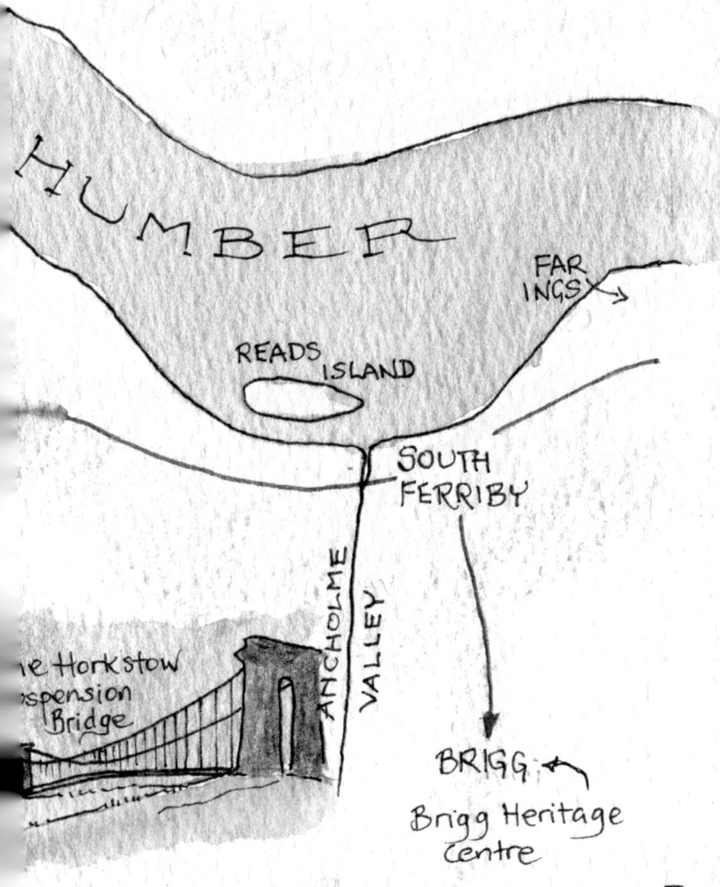

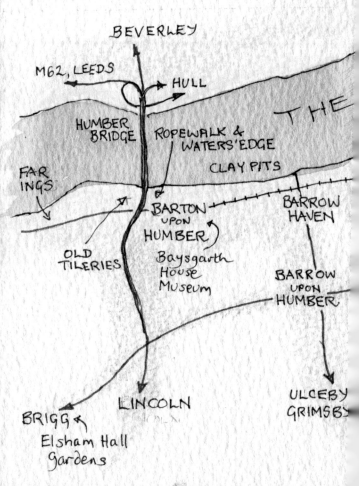

SKETCH MAP continued

BEVERLEY

M62, LEEDS

HULL

HUMBER BRIDGE

ROPEWALK & WATERS' EDGE

THE

CLAY PITS

FAR INGS

BARTON UPON HUMBER

BARROW HAVEN

OLD TILERIES

Baysgarth House Museum

BARROW UPON HUMBER

LINCOLN

ULCEBY GRIMSBY

BRIGG

Elsham Hall Gardens

4

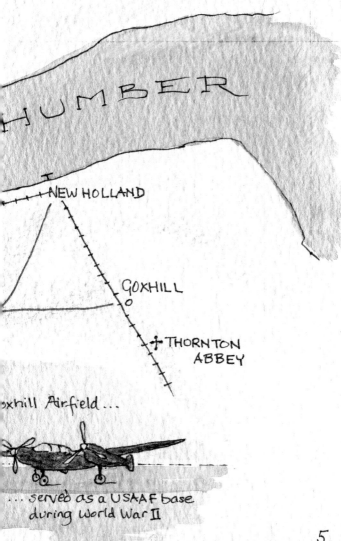

HUMBER

New Holland

GOXHILL
O

✝ THORNTON
ABBEY

...oxhill Airfield...

... served as a USAAF base
during World War II

5

HUMBER VESSELS

Humber Sloop

The Humber sloop was designed
to sail in open estuary waters and to
make some coastal voyages. They
handled bulk cargoes such as farm
produce, coal, cement, chalk, bricks
and tiles. In the summer they might
trade as far as London to the South
and the Tyne to the North.
In 1981, the restored sloop Amy
Howson became the first sloop to
sail the Humber in more than thirty
years.

HUMBER VESSELS

Humber Keel

The Humber keels were used for inshore & inland cargo transport around Hull and the Humber Estuary. They were designed to work in shallow waters so they could be used on the waterways connected to the Humber. Like sloops, they would carry local goods. All the sailing keels had gone by 1948 but one has been returned to sail by the Humber Keel and Sloop Preservation Society.

HUMBER VESSELS

P.S Lincoln Castle

The Lincoln Castle was a coal-fired
paddle steamer which operated
as a car and passenger ferry
between New Holland and Hull
from 1940s until 1978. She was
the last coal-fired paddle-steamer
in regular service and could
carry up to 20 cars and 1,200
passengers. Although ferries
were sometimes stranded on
sandbanks, the service was
much used until the opening of
the Humber Bridge made ferries
obsolete.

COOLING TOWERS

Beyond the Humber's edge
Cooling towers stand
Squat & powerful

Like the castles
Which stood against invaders,
Whose lords ruled our lives,
Levied our labour,
Our barley and our oats,
Took liberties
And, now and then, our wives.

The cooling towers
Represent a different power,
Guarding against cold TV dinners,
Sour milk and silent rooms...
And exact, quiet and sure,
Different kinds of taxes
As their gases
Leak and stain
Our future.

© Trevor Millum 1998

9

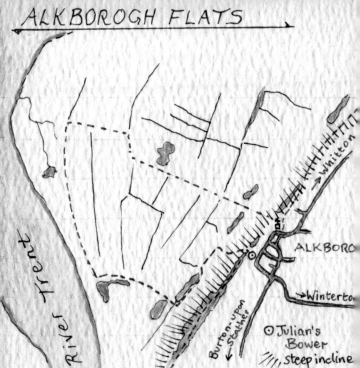

Alkborough Flats, where the rivers
Trent and Ouse join to form the Humber,
is part of a managed realignment project
where, in 2006, the river defences were
deliberately breached, allowing the
Humber to flood over 400 acres of
fields. Habitat management since
then has created a range of habitats,

10

including extensive reed-beds, lagoons and saltmarsh. It's a haven for wading birds and wildfowl, hence an ideal area for birdwatchers and walkers. The village of Alk- borough sits high above the Flats on the cliff top.

There are a number of interesting walks in the area. A circular route from Julian's Bower takes you down the escarpment onto the Flats, from where you can walk along the em- bankment and then back along a lane and up the hill to the village.

A walk south through a wooded path will take you above the Flats to Burton-upon-Stather and then to Flixborough. Going North along the ridge you will arrive at the small riverside village of Whitton, via the 'Devil's Causeway'.

A detailed guide to the circular walk can be found on N. Lincs Council site.

JULIAN'S BOWER.

Both the name and the origin of this turf maze at Alkborough ~ or, more accurately, a labyrinth, as it has a single entrance & path (you can't get lost!) are the subject of much speculation.

The maze overlooks the meeting point of the Ouse and Trent, with an earthwork known as Countess Close above it.

Some think that the feature is of Roman origin and others that it was cut by monks. It may well have been used by the Medieval church for religious purposes and reverted to its former use as an amusement after the Reformation.

The early Christian church did use the idea of mazes as symbolic of the path to heaven, and also as a penitential device.

The nearby church has a copy
of the maze inlaid into the floor
of the porch and there is also a
copy in the east window.

There is another copy of the
design in the stone cross marking
one of the graves.

Julian's Bower Turf 'Maze'

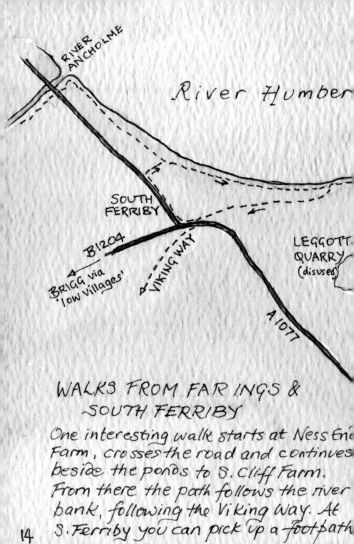

RIVER ANCHOLME

River Humber

SOUTH FERRIBY

B1204

BRIGG via 'low villages'

VIKING WAY

LEGGOTT QUARRY (disused)

A 1077

WALKS FROM FARINGS & SOUTH FERRIBY

One interesting walk starts at Ness End Farm, crosses the road and continues beside the ponds to S. Cliff Farm. From there the path follows the river bank, following the Viking Way. At S. Ferriby you can pick up a footpath

14

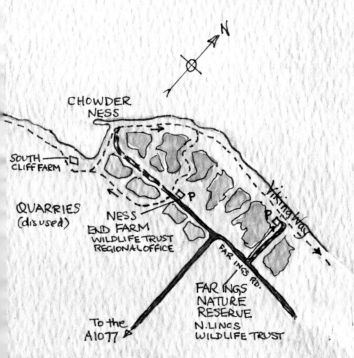

leading back to the river, passing
Chowder Ness and returning to the
start through the Reserve. A
longer walk would involve going
to the Ancholme and following
the river – or there's all of the Viking
Way!

15

HIDING

If you think there's nothing going on
You're wrong
If you think everyone & everything is gone
You're wrong
Just hush
And in a moment's silence
You will hear the song
Of blackbird and thrush
And then – is that a wren
So quickly come and gone?
Wildfowl are waiting in the reeds
And of course throughout the site
There are germinating seeds + bulbs
And all they need is
Just a little bit of sun
  Ah – all is quiet again
  Be still
  You won't have to wait for long
If you think there's nothing
                    going on
You're wrong

16   © Trevor Millum 2016

FAR INGS NATIONAL NATURE RESERVE

'Ings' is an O. English word for the wet pastures to the west of Barton. Before the embankment was built, they were part of the Humber flood plain.

Since Roman times, the underlying clay has been used to make bricks and tiles. This industry flourished in the 19th century until the clay began to run out around 1950.

The clay pits flooded and became a haven for wildlife. In 1983 the area was purchased by the Lincolnshire Wildlife Trust and through its management is now even richer in a wide range of wildlife.

There are footpaths through the reserve, bird hides and a Visitor Centre from which views over the pits, reedbeds, estuary and Humber Bridge can be enjoyed. Check the website for opening times.

17

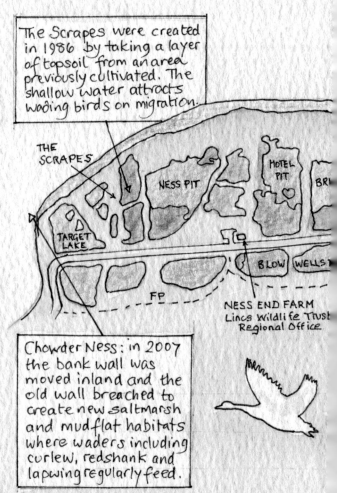

The Scrapes were created in 1986 by taking a layer of topsoil from an area previously cultivated. The shallow water attracts wading birds on migration.

THE SCRAPES

NESS PIT

HOTEL PIT

BRI

TARGET LAKE

BLOW WELLS

FP

NESS END FARM
Lincs Wildlife Trust
Regional Office

Chowder Ness: in 2007 the bank wall was moved inland and the old wall breached to create new saltmarsh and mudflat habitats where waders including curlew, redshank and lapwing regularly feed.

The Humber: wildfowl are abundant in the estuary and the foreshore mud supports wading birds.

FAR INGS VISITOR CENTRE

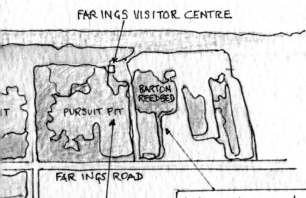

PURSUIT PIT

BARTON REEDBED

FAR INGS ROAD

The freshwater lakes are rich in microscopic life, providing food for invertebrates, which in turn support fish. Heron, grebes and kingfishers prey on the fish & duck nest on the islands and margins.

Old meadow and scrub provide sheltered sunny corners for butterflies & the hawthorn is a good nesting habitat for small birds. In May the grassland is dotted with a variety of wildflowers

w. lincstrust. org. uk /far-ings-visitor-centre

19

THE HUMBER RUMBA ⟶

We live along the Humber
We do the Humber Rumba
Humba Rumba!
The river never slumbers
Cooler than cucumber —
Let's hear it for the Humber!

It's breezy on the river
East winds make you shiver
We don't care
We don't mind
We like it there
Like what we find
On the edge of Mother Humber
Doing the Humber Rumba!

We visit Cleethorpes beach
The sea is out of reach
We don't mind
Like what we find
At the end of Mother Humber
Doing the Humber Rumba!

The Bridge is fine ~ and large
You can view it free of charge
It's very nice
Now they've cut the price
But we're not going far
We like it where we are
On the banks of Mother Humber
Doing the Humba Rumba!

It's a long way from the City
They may look at us with pity
But we don't care
We don't mind
We like it rain or shine
Here along the Humber
Doing the HUMBA RUMBA!

© Trevor Millum 2001

21

WILDERSPIN NATIONAL
── SCHOOL ──➤

Samuel Wilderspin (1791-1866) is one
of the founding fathers of modern
education. He believed in learning
through experience, the importance
of play and of encouragement rather
than punishment.

When Wilderspin moved to Barton, he
created his own model Infant School
on Queen Street, complete with playground. The school became a base
for the promotion of progressive
education throughout Britain.

The school, built in 1844, is the
only known surviving Wilderspin
school and playground. He helped
to design and equip it and taught
here for several years.

English Heritage recognize the
school as one of the most important in England - both for
its unique links with Wilderspin
and for its importance as a
design for other Victorian schools

and a model example of an enlightened form of schooling that spread throughout the world.

The school was in use until 1978 when staff and pupils moved to new premises. The building was

in a bad state of repair and there were moves to have it demolished. However, more enlightened views prevailed and a Preservation Trust was formed leading to the rescue of the building which is now an important heritage site.

23

THE ROPEWALK

Once a busy rope-making factory and important local employer, the Ropewalk is now a cultural hub.

GARDEN | GALLERY | RECEPTION & SHOP

An unusual, low maintenance dry garden with raised beds, shrubs and grasses as well as sculptures and found objects.

Main entrance reception & shop selling work by local and national artists: includ ceramics, prints textiles, jeweller and cards.

Exhibition space with regularly changing displays in a range of art forms.

24

NOT TO SCALE

The Ropewalk Café, popular for drinks, light meals and, most of all, cakes!

...TORY OF THE ROPERY

CAFÉ

The Museum area tells the story of the Ropewalk. Rope-making was a local cottage industry here, serving Hull and the many users of the Humber. Hall's Ropery was established in 1803 and built up a reputation for quality which lasted for over 150 years. Ropes made here were used by Hunt's Everest expedition in 1953. The Ropery closed in 1989. The Museum chronicles the lives of those who worked here as well as the technical developments in rope-making.

25

Further gallery space, also with regularly changing exhibitions.

ALLERY

Where huge lengths of rope were once stretched and coiled, there are now rooms serving as artists' studios, meeting areas and office accommodation.

The old despatch building, now a health and beauty business.

26

..... FOR A QUARTER OF A MILE

This end of the building is usually accessed via Maltkiln Road or from the paths along the Humber Bank.

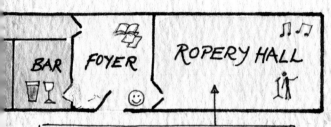

Ropery Hall is a performance space seating over a hundred people. It has a comprehensive programme of drama, music, comedy and film - and draws audiences from a wide area north and south of the river.

The Ropewalk also hosts courses, provides packs for schools and sells publications on local history.

www.the-ropewalk.co.uk

Events at Ropery Hall:
www.roperyhall.co.uk

Sonnet for The Ropewalk

Imagine... returning from the river,
Rope-makers can detect faint melodies.
The notes float on the air. They rise
                    and cease
And then begin again. A ghostly shiver
                                    all.
~Some kind of premonition ~ quietens
But then the usual working pace resumes:
Hands turn to sisal and manila, combs
Tease out the waste, twines stretch
                    and muscles pull.
In Ropery Hall, gathered from near
                              and far
An audience sits patiently and
Waits for musicians tuning guitars,
                              hands
Unsullied by the rough handshake of tar.
The lights go down. All's quiet. Music.
                         These now
The only strings & cords the building
                              knows.

WATERS' EDGE VISITOR CENTRE

Once the site of brick and tile works,
this area has seen many changes.
From the 1950s there was a chemical
plant here, resulting in a site which
was badly contaminated. It was taken
over by N. Lincolnshire Council in 1996,
the top layers of soil removed and new
soil from Far Ings Reserve brought in.
The area was converted into a Country
Park and the eco-friendly Visitor
Centre was opened in 2006.

WATERS' EDGE COUNTRY PARK

The Park comprises 110 acres (44.5 hectares) of woodland, wetland and wildflower meadows, split over two sites. There are two Site of Special Scientific Interest (SSSI), ten ponds, native woodlands and a number of walks through the trees and around the ponds. The sketch opposite gives a rough idea of these; an accurate map can be obtained from the Centre.

Across the Haven, by the Humber Bridge viewing area, there are further wildflower meadows and woodland.

The Humber supports a huge amount of wildlife. Wild-fowl occur in great numbers and wading birds inhabit the mud of the foreshore. The freshwater ponds and lakes formed from the old clay pits provide another key habitat for wildlife.

River Humber

WATERS' EDGE COUNTRY PARK

FISHING LAKES

EAST POND

BIG POND

WATERS EDGE VISITOR CENTRE

HUMBER BRIDGE VIEWING AREA

CAR PARK

CAR PARK

ROPE WALK

RAILWAY

STATION

FARINGS RD.

HUMBER BRIDGE

THE OLD TILERIES

A15

31

HUMBER TILERIES

Clay has been extracted for brick and tile making since the 18th century. At one point there were well over a dozen companies operating along the Humber bank between S. Ferriby and New Holland. There were other scattered workings further West. By the 1970s much of the clay had been extracted and the majority of works had closed down.

The clay pits, having filled with fresh water, serve a variety of uses today, including sailing, water skiing, fishing and wild-life reserves, managed by Lincoln shire Wildlife Trust.

One of the longest established firms is that of William Blyth, which still produces tiles at Hoe

Hill and Far Ings. At the Far
Ings site, the Old Tile Works
includes a coffee shop and
restaurant, artisan craft units
and is home to a herd of Hereford
Shorthorn cattle.

WEST MARSH STROLL →

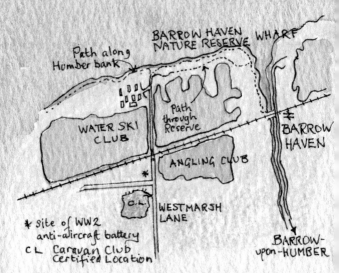

BARROW HAVEN
NATURE RESERVE WHARF

Path along
Humber bank

WATER SKI
CLUB

Path
through
Reserve

BARROW
HAVEN

ANGLING CLUB

C.L. WESTMARSH
LANE

＊ site of WW2
anti-aircraft battery
C L Caravan Club
Certified Location

BARROW-
upon-HUMBER

From Barrow Haven, cross over the railway and walk along the west side of
the Beck towards the river. You will
see a path to the left at the bottom
of a steep grassy bank. A gate marks
the entrance to B.H. Nature Reserve.
Take the path through the reserve
along the edge of the reed-fringed
pond, which emerges near the Water
Ski Club. You can continue along
the Humber bank west or return to B.H.

SWIFTS!

We've learnt to seize the time,
                   and grab those few
warm moments before the sun decides
                        to hide
in clouds or sink behind the next door roof,
hear the blackbird splashing on the
                        pond side
as if he's not bathed for days, smell
                        elberflower –
and then – look up! Hurrah! The swifts
                   are back.
At first, a few high specks, then more –
                   and lower
still, and never still, these Xs of black
swoop past our tiles, between the
                   chimney stacks.
Excited by the dusk, off out with mates,
like teens on aerial joy rides, in tight
                        packs,
they circle and jostle, out to
                        celebrate;
except those special pairs whom we
                        receive
and welcome once more to nest
                   beneath our eaves.

JOHN HARRISON

No description of this part of the country would be complete without a mention of John Harrison (1693-1776) clockmaker extraordinary, who lived and worked in Barrow-upon-Humber for the first half of his long life. A carpenter who taught himself mechanics, amongst other topics, he became an innovative constructor of clocks & watches who eventually solved the 'problem of Longitude' with his marine chronometer design.

While still young, he, with his brother James, made several long-case clocks of great accuracy and also supplied the stable block clock to the Earl of Yarborough. After 300 years, that clock at Brocklesby is still keeping good time.

As well as innovations in clock design, such as the grasshopper escapement, the caged roller bearing and grid-iron pendulum, he invented the bimetallic strip, which is in use in all manner of modern devices, from kettles to irons.

A true genius, he is commemorated with a plaque in Westminster Abbey and his wonderful clocks can be seen at the Royal Observatory in Greenwich. His portrait hangs in Barrow church, together with an explanatory display.

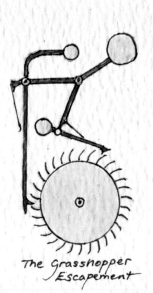

The Grasshopper Escapement

PAPIST HALL

This striking building on Barrow's High Street is one of the village's oldest houses. It dates from the mid-17th century when it was fashionable to build in brick and tile rather than

timber frame and thatch. It was built as one house with the original entrance in the middle. The raised brick pier shows where the main door was. To the right is a window that was put into that opening. The door would have led into an entrance hall

38

with a chimney and ingle-nook fireplace.
There would have been a large room
on each side.

The house was built for William Brox-
holme, who owned one of the three
manors of Barrow and was later MP
for Grimsby. The name 'Papist Hall'
probably refers to a mid-18th century
owner, John Pannell, a Roman Catholic
merchant from Brigg. It was later
divided into three dwellings, at which
point the original central doorway
became a window, and the windows
themselves were enlarged.

The building fell into disrepair and
was rescued in the 1970s and care-
fully restored. At that point the
dwellings were given their fanciful
names, e.g. Abbot's Abode, which
bear no relation to historical fact.

THORNTON ABBEY

THORNTON ABBEY GATEHOUSE

Though little remains of Thornton Abbey,
the Gatehouse still stands. It is an
imposing structure and would have been
even more impressive when it was built in
the 14th century. There are three floor
which can be explored, including two
large rooms and a number of intriguing
passageways. In the care of English Heritage

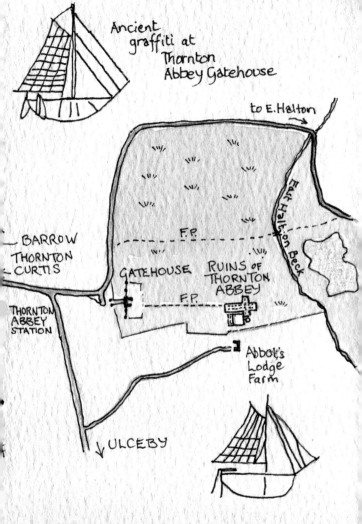

Ancient
graffiti at
Thornton
Abbey Gatehouse

to E. Halton

Fax Halton Beck

F.P.

BARROW
THORNTON
CURTIS

GATEHOUSE

RUINS OF
THORNTON
ABBEY

F.P.

THORNTON
ABBEY
STATION

Abbot's
Lodge
Farm

↓ ULCEBY

41

A SIMPLE CROSSWORD

ACROSS CLUES

5. Go through it, in it or up it at T.A.

6. Never amateur at Ropery Hall

7. To be seen on many a Reserve pond

8. Though Far, they are quite near!

DOWN CLUES

1. Harrison's home town.

2. No longer heard at St. Peter's.

3. Gave his name to a bower.

4. Would be held upstairs at
                    5 across.

▷ ANSWERS ON PAGE 46

A LITTLE RIDDLE

My first is in Barton but not in Barrow
My 2nd is in wide but not in narrow
My 3rd is in dangerous but not in anger
My 4th is in sausage & also in banger
I go in and out with no gates or doors
On the Humber they know me of old —
                    that's for sure!

43

A GREEN MAN MAZE

This is a maze, not a labyrinth.

© Trevor Millum 2016

Can you find a way from the mouth to the nose? And from the nose to the left eye?

44

FINDING OUT MORE.

The easiest way to find out more
is by investigating websites. Here
are some I've found useful. And
if I sound like a spokesman for
N. Lincs Tourism, I'm not - I just
like it here.

Waters' Edge Country Park and
Visitor Centre, together with
lots of other information about
the area: www.visitnorthlincolnshire.com

Far Ings Nature Reserve:
www.lincstrust.org.uk

The Ropewalk:
www.the-ropewalk.co.uk

Thornton Abbey:
www.english-heritage.org.uk

John Harrison's clocks - and much more:
www.rmg.co.uk

Wilderspin School:
www.wilderspinschool.org.uk

Papist Hall and more about Barrow-
upon-Humber's heritage:
www.betterbarrow.org

Humber Vessels:
> www.keelsandsloops.org.uk

The Old Tile Works:
> www.theoldtileworks.com

Also of interest:

www.briggheritage.org — interestin
heritage centre with unique
preserved Iron Age raft.

www.facebook.com/normonbyhall
park, stately home, walled garden
and farming museum.

www.facebook.com/northlincsmuseum
a good local museum including
excellent Roman mosaics.

www.facebook.com/2021VisualArts
high quality exhibitions in a converted church, now an art space.

CROSSWORD ANSWERS:
1. BARROW 2. SERMON 3. JULIAN
4. FEASTS 5. GATEHOUSE 6. DRAMATICS
7. SWAN 8. INGS   RIDDAE : TIDE

46